Henry O. Flipper

Kathryn Browne Pfeifer

Twenty-First Century Books

A Division of Henry Holt and Company   New York

The author wishes to thank Irsle King and Ray MacColl for their invaluable help.

PHOTO CREDITS
cover: flag by Fred J. Eckert/FPG International; photo courtesy U.S. Military Academy Library. **3:** U. S. Military Academy Archives. **4:** U.S. Military Academy Library. **8:** Fort Davis National Historic Site. **9:** National Archives. **12, 13:** Ray MacColl. **16:** Schomburg Center for Research in Black Culture/NYPL. **18:** Atlanta Historical Society. **20,21:** Ray MacColl. **25, 26, 31, 34:** U. S. Military Academy Library. **37, 38:** National Archives. **40:** Fort Sill Museum. **44:** Fort Concho National Historic Landmark. **45:** Arizona Historical Society/Tucson #19748. **50, 52, 53:** Fort Davis National Historic Site. **57, 63:** Ray MacColl. **68:** Ruvén Afanador. **71:** Fort Davis National Historic Site. **73:** Steve Wilson.

npany, Inc.

New York, NY 10011

Henry Holt ® and colophon are registered trademarks of Henry Holt and Company, Inc.
Publishers since 1866

Library of Congress Cataloging-in-Publication Data

Pfeifer, Kathryn.
Henry O. Flipper / Kathryn Pfeifer. — 1st ed.
p.   cm. — (African-American soldiers)
Includes bibliographical references and index.
Summary: Examines the life of the first African-American graduate of West Point, including his dishonorable discharge from the Army which was reversed nearly 100 years later.
1. Flipper, Henry Ossian, 1856-1940—Juvenile literature. 2. United States. Army—Biography—Juvenile literature. 3. Soldiers—United States—Biography—Juvenile literature. 4. Afro-American soldiers—United States—Biography—Juvenile literature. 5. United States. Army—Afro-Americans—History—19th century—Juvenile literature.
[1. Flipper, Henry Ossian, 1856-1940. 2. Soldiers.
3. Afro-Americans—Biography.]
I. Title. II. Series.
U53.F55P44   1993
355'.0089'96073—dc20   [B]   93-10631   CIP   AC

ISBN 0-8050-2351-8
First Edition—1993

Printed in the United States of America
All first editions are printed on acid-free paper ∞.

10 9 8 7 6 5 4 3 2 1

Contents

Chapter 1
The Path of Uprightness

As the summer sun disappeared over the mountains on August 13, 1881, most of the soldiers stationed at the small Texas outpost called Fort Davis found relief from the day's heat. However, one soldier was not as fortunate. Second Lieutenant Henry Ossian Flipper, the United States Army's only black officer, sat locked inside a small, windowless cell in the guardhouse. The fort's commander, Colonel William R. Shafter, had arrested him that afternoon for allegedly embezzling government funds.

Four years earlier, Henry Flipper had received national recognition for being the first African American to graduate from the United States Military Academy at West Point. It was a tremendous accomplishment for a young man who had been born into slavery.

Cadet Henry Ossian Flipper

Although life at the academy had been difficult and lonely, Flipper had been determined not to let his skin color stand in the way of his becoming an officer. Whenever anyone insulted him, he tried to prove to himself that it wasn't done because of his color. "If I could find such a reason," he explained, "I [was] disposed not only to overlook the offense, but to forgive and forget it."

This was an attitude that served Flipper well, and when he graduated in 1877, he said that it was "not color of face, but color of character alone" that had triumphed. Flipper's commission as a second lieutenant assigned to Troop A of the 10th United States Cavalry was proof that African Americans could succeed at West Point.

The 10th Cavalry was one of several army units made up of African-American soldiers that had been formed at the end of the Civil War. The men of the 9th and 10th Cavalries, and the 24th and 25th Infantries, eventually became known as "Buffalo Soldiers," named by the Indians because the black soldiers' dark skin and curly hair reminded them of buffalo. It was a nickname the men were proud of; they knew the buffalo was an important part of the Indians' culture.

Second Lieutenant Flipper's first assignment

was Fort Sill, Indian Territory (now part of Oklahoma), where he met up with his troop. Shortly after his arrival, he noted in his journal, "I haven't experienced any thing but happiness. I am not isolated. I am not ostracized by a single officer." Flipper spent most of that first year helping to keep peace between the Indians and settlers.

From Fort Sill, Henry Flipper followed his troop to posts in Texas, where they set up telegraph lines, built roads, and surveyed government lands. In the fall of 1880, Flipper was transferred to Fort Davis, where he was put in charge of supplies and equipment for the entire post. As always, Flipper felt confident that he would win the respect of his fellow officers and the black soldiers he commanded.

Now, however, in the sweltering darkness of his cramped cell, Flipper's past accomplishments and hard-earned respect seemed worlds away.

After four days of confinement, on the evening of August 17, Colonel Shafter released Lieutenant Flipper to his quarters. Shafter had confiscated many of Flipper's belongings and had limited Flipper's freedom by ordering a guard to stand watch over his quarters day and night. Flipper found his treatment humiliating. He knew that no

Fort Davis, Texas

other officer accused of a similar crime would have been degraded in such a manner.

Colonel Shafter seemed intent on persecuting Henry Flipper and soon brought court-martial charges against the bright, young lieutenant. These charges were to change Flipper's life forever.

On December 8, 1881, Lieutenant Flipper was

found innocent of embezzlement, yet guilty of "conduct unbecoming an officer and gentleman." He was sentenced to be dishonorably discharged from the United States Army, and six months later, in 1882, Flipper left the military for good. Flipper later wrote, " . . . never did a man walk the path of uprightness straighter than I did, but the trap was cunningly laid and I was sacrificed."

Although upset and frustrated over the outcome of the trial, Henry Flipper did not let the situation get the best of him. A lesser man might have crumbled, yet Flipper's indomitable spirit could not be broken. The following July he headed northwest to El Paso, Texas, to begin his life anew.

Over the next forty-eight years, Henry Flipper applied what he had learned at West Point and made a name for himself in the fields of surveying and engineering, all the while proving to himself and others that he was a confident, trustworthy, responsible individual. He held many important positions, which included special agent for the United States Department of Justice and interpreter for the Senate Committee on Foreign Relations.

Even so, the ex-lieutenant never gave up his crusade to see justice done. He wanted his dishonorable discharge overturned, reinstating him

Colonel William R. Shafter

9

to active service with the United States Army. Those who knew Flipper knew that, while he was achieving terrific success as a civilian, he still thought of himself first as an army officer, and second as a surveyor and engineer.

In 1930, Flipper retired at the age of seventy-four. Some people say Henry Flipper accomplished more than he ever would have had he been able to stay in the military. And indeed, his career, spent mainly outside the United States, was varied, highly productive, and distinguished. Yet on April 26, 1940, the first black graduate of West Point died a forgotten soldier and a forgotten African-American hero.

It wasn't until the mid-1970s that someone attempted to clear Flipper's name, once and for all. Ray MacColl, a white schoolteacher from Georgia, challenged the Army Board for Correction of Military Records to reverse Flipper's dishonorable discharge. In December 1976, the board finally acknowledged that the military had mishandled Flipper's case, and granted Second Lieutenant Henry Ossian Flipper an honorable discharge.

Although Henry Flipper never lived to see his rank and duty restored, his early accomplishments in overcoming racial barriers at the United States Military Academy were not lost on other African-American soldiers. It was Henry Ossian Flipper who had set a standard of excellence for all future African-American soldiers to follow.

Chapter 2

Freedom and Education

In southwest Georgia, less than twenty miles from the Florida border, in the small town of Thomasville, Henry Ossian Flipper was born into slavery on March 21, 1856. He would be the oldest of five boys born into the Flipper family. For the first two years of his life, Henry lived with his mother, Isabella Buckhalter, while his father, Festus Flipper, already a skilled shoemaker, traveled to Virginia to serve an apprenticeship under a carriage maker. Festus returned to Thomasville in 1858, and a year later Henry's brother Joseph was born. But soon after Joseph's birth, Festus was faced with a dilemma.

Henry's parents were owned by different people. His mother, his brother, and he belonged to the Reverend Reuben H. Lucky, while his father was the property of Ephraim G. Ponder. This

Isabella Buckhalter

arrangement had worked well until Ponder announced that he was going to move his family and slaves to the northern Georgia city of Atlanta, more than two hundred miles away. Although Festus had some savings of his own, he was not permitted to buy his family outright from Reverend Lucky. Instead, he had to persuade his owner to buy them. In fact, Festus Flipper lent Ephraim Ponder the money to do so.

Festus Flipper

With the family intact, Henry, his parents, and his brother Joseph moved to Atlanta, to a twenty-five-acre farm Ponder had recently purchased. Unlike most slaves of that time, Henry's father was a respected craftsman, who contracted his work out and paid a portion of his wages to his owner. As Henry remembered, "These bond people were . . . virtually free. They acquired and accumulated wealth, lived happily . . . . " The only two things that they truly needed, conceded Henry, were "absolute freedom and education."

Elsewhere in Georgia and throughout the country, other slaves were not as lucky as the Flippers. Many toiled from dawn to dusk in cotton fields across the South and lived, as one slave woman recalled, like dogs. "If they caught us with a piece of paper in our pockets, they'd whip us," the woman explained. "They was afraid we'd learn to read and write . . . . "

Over a thirty-year period, the number of slaves in the United States doubled to four million by 1860. In the meantime, the nation was becoming increasingly divided over many issues, one of which was slavery. The northern states were more industrial and depended less on slavery than the southern states did. The South, more agricultural than the North, depended heavily on slave labor. By 1861, the nation became embroiled in a bitter civil war over Union and state's rights.

From the beginning of the Civil War, many slaves in the South realized that freedom lay to the north, and soon hundreds of slaves were trying to reach Union lines. Legally, Union officers were permitted to free only those slaves who had worked for the Confederate Army. All other slaves could be returned to their owners, but many weren't. It wasn't until July 1862 that Congress passed a law freeing all slaves belonging to owners who supported the Confederacy. In that same month, Congress also allowed blacks to enlist in the military, thereby enabling thousands of black men to permanently gain their freedom.

However, many people were afraid of putting guns in the hands of former slaves; some people who thought that blacks were an inferior race also thought they would not be competent on the battlefield. The June 7, 1863, skirmish at Milliken's Bend, Louisiana, proved otherwise. On that day, 1,500 Confederates attacked a small Union troop made up of both white and black soldiers. When the battle was over, Union officers no longer doubted the fighting abilities of black soldiers. As one officer wrote, "The bravery of the blacks at Milliken's Bend completely revolutionized the sentiment of the army with regard to the employment of Negro troops."

An escaped slave in the Union Army

One month later, six hundred recruits in the all-black 54th Massachusetts Infantry showed unshakable courage when they stormed the Confederate position at Fort Wagner, South Carolina, knowing full well that they might die. By the time the fighting was over, the unit had lost half of its men.

Rallying slaves to fight, Frederick Douglass, a powerful orator and a former slave, declared, "The arm of the slaves [is] the best defense against the arm of the slaveholder . . . . I urge you to fly to arms . . . . This is your golden opportunity."

The effect was amazing. More than 180,000 blacks answered Douglass's call, and eventually 166 black regiments formed the United States Colored Troops to fight for the Union. Yet during the entire war, fewer than 100 black officers were commissioned.

By the end of the war, some 37,000 black soldiers had lost their lives, but the deeds of black soldiers were not forgotten. There were 16 Congressional Medal of Honor recipients from the colored troops, and, for the first time, Congress authorized the formation of six black peacetime army regiments—the 9th and 10th Cavalries and the 38th, 39th, 40th, and 41st Infantries. (The latter four regiments would be combined in 1869 to become the 24th and 25th Infantries.)

Up until 1864, the war seemed to have had little effect on the Flippers. Mr. Ponder, their owner, had separated from his wife, leaving her in charge as mistress over the slaves and the farm. Their mistress permitted one of the slaves to open a night school for the slave children. And so, eight-year-old Henry began his education. "And the first book [I] ever studied—I dare say ever saw—was a confederate reprint of Webster's *Blueback Speller*," recalled Henry. But his schooling was soon interrupted.

The Ponder house in Atlanta, bombarded by Sherman's troops after the slaves and their mistress fled to Macon

By the early summer of 1864, the war became real for the Flippers and their mistress. General Sherman and his Union troops were advancing closer and closer toward Atlanta, forcing many families to leave the area. To avoid attack the Flippers, along with the rest of the Ponders' slaves, followed their mistress to the town of Macon, 103 miles southeast of Atlanta. Luckily, Macon was spared the destruction that befell Atlanta.

In the spring of 1865, after a nine-month stay in Macon, Festus Flipper decided to return to Atlanta with his family. The war was over. On April 9, 1865, Confederate General Robert E. Lee formally surrendered to Union General Ulysses S. Grant. The end of the war also signaled an end to slavery. Later that year, Congress ratified the 13th Amendment to the Constitution, abolishing slavery.

"Atlanta was in ruins," Henry recalled, "and it appeared a dreary place indeed to start anew on the unfinished journey of life. Every thing was not destroyed, however . . . . The people were rapidly returning, and the railroads . . . were rapidly being rebuilt." Opportunities abounded in the city, and Henry's father set up a shoe shop on Decatur Street. His next task was finding a tutor for Henry

Festus Flipper and family in the doorway of his shoe shop

and his brother Joseph. Luckily, he didn't have to look far.

Shortly after arriving in Atlanta, the Flippers became friendly with their neighbors, an ex-rebel captain and his wife. When the wife offered to instruct the boys for a small fee, the Flippers jumped at the chance. Although Isabella and

A young Henry
Flipper

Festus Flipper required each of their sons to learn and master a trade—either shoemaking or carriage making—they understood the importance of education. So at an early age, Henry was encouraged in his studies and instilled with a desire to learn.

After a year of private instruction, the Flipper boys enrolled in one of the newly opened American

Missionary Association schools for blacks. And a few years later, they went on to Atlanta University to continue their studies.

It wasn't until the fall of 1872, as Flipper recalled, that the idea of attending West Point entered his mind. One day while sitting in his father's shoe shop, Henry overheard that the cadet from his district would soon be graduating, leaving a vacant slot. Then and there, he became determined to be the one to fill that vacancy.

Henry Flipper had several advantages: he was determined, persistent, educated, and healthy—and it was an election year. The Republican nominee for Congress from his district was elected that fall, and by January 1873, Flipper had already made contact with his new congressman, James Crawford Freeman.

Every individual seeking to enter West Point must be appointed by an elected United States government official—a congressman, senator, the president, or vice president. Knowing this and knowing that his congressman was newly elected, Henry made sure to write to him as soon as he took office.

By March 22, 1873, Congressman Freeman contacted Flipper by letter, saying that, "as you were the first applicant, I am disposed to give you the first chance; but the requirements are rigid and strict . . . . If after reading them you think you can undergo the examination without doubt, I will nominate you." By April 5, Henry had met all the requirements and was appointed by Congressman Freeman to West Point.

After he had gotten his appointment, several local newspapers in Atlanta wanted to interview Henry. He declined such attention. "My chief reason for objecting," he later wrote, "was merely this: I feared some evil might befall me while passing through Georgia *en route* for West Point, if too great a knowledge of me should precede me." However, a short article did appear, and a few days later, a white gentleman pulled Flipper aside in the local post office and tried to buy Henry's appointment for his son for $5,000. "This I refused instantly," Henry recalled. "I had so set my mind on West Point that, having the appointment, neither threats nor excessive bribes could induce me to relinquish it . . . . I afterward had reason to believe the offer was made merely to test me."

When May came, Henry set off for the United States Military Academy at West Point, New York, situated on the bank of the Hudson River.

"I had so set my mind on West Point that, having the appointment, neither threats nor excessive bribes could induce me to relinquish it . . . ."

Chapter 3

A Bittersweet Experience

Henry's first view of West Point was from the deck of a ferry boat that shuttled passengers back and forth from the town of Garrison, on the east bank of the Hudson River, to West Point. As he looked across the river at the gray stone buildings on the afternoon of May 20, 1873, he "shuddered." He knew that the next four years would be an uphill battle, both physically and mentally.

Once ashore, Henry reported to the adjutant's office and began his life as a "plebe," as all new candidates were called. Afterward, he was led to the barracks; a walk, that in his words, "was certainly not very encouraging." He remembered, "The rear windows were crowded with cadets watching my unpretending passage . . . [to the] barracks with apparently as much astonishment and interest as they would . . . have watched Hannibal crossing the Alps. Their words, jeers . . . were most insulting."

A cadet room at West Point, 1877, arranged in proper military order

Later that day after dinner, Plebe Flipper was given a half hour to unpack and get his room in military order. This meant he had to follow a long list of instructions on how to arrange his room. His bed had to be positioned against the side and back walls, with his mattress, bed sheets, and pillow folded neatly on top. And his clothes, down to the socks, had to be put away in a particular order.

When a senior cadet stopped by to inspect Flipper's room, he wasn't pleased with what Flipper had done. He threw everything on the floor and ordered Henry to arrange his room again. After three attempts, Henry finally managed to please the cadet and was left alone for the rest of the night.

Reflecting on his first day at West Point, Henry remembered, "What I had seen and experienced ... filled me with fear and apprehension. I expected every moment to be insulted or struck.... I was uneasy and miserable, ever thinking of the regulations, verbal and written, which had been given to me. How they haunted me! I kept repeating them over and over, fearful lest I might forget and violate them, and be dismissed."

Henry Flipper was the sixth African American to be appointed to West Point, and after reading about the trials of the black cadets before him— none of whom had succeeded in graduating—he fully expected a rough time at the academy. Surprisingly though, he later learned that the treatment he received on his first day was no more severe than that of other plebes. Everyone was going through the same ordeal of arranging their rooms just so and then having a cadet come by and upset everything. It was all part of being a plebe and learning to take orders and respect superiors.

On his second day at West Point, Flipper received a letter from an upperclassman, Cadet James Webster Smith, who was among the first five African Americans appointed to West Point. At the time of Flipper's arrival, Smith was the only African American remaining at the academy. The letter was a complete surprise because Henry had been told back in Atlanta that Smith had been dismissed. Yet Smith's letter was not encouraging. In it, Smith advised Henry that if he had any hopes of graduating, he would be wise to keep to himself and not argue with any of his white classmates. Failure to do this had been Smith's downfall from the beginning. Unlike Henry, Smith was a fighter and had a difficult time enduring abuse silently.

Five days later, another African-American candidate, John Williams, arrived at West Point from Virginia. Henry Flipper was instructed to show Williams "the ropes," which he did, later commenting that "his first days at West Point were much more pleasant than mine had been."

By the 28th of May, all one hundred new

candidates had reported, and for the next three days, everyone was tested in grammar, history, geography, orthography (spelling), reading, and mathematics. Those that passed their examinations would remain plebes at West Point, those that failed would be sent home. "It was a fearful moment," Henry said, recalling the day the passing names were read. "I stood motionless while the order was being read until I heard my name . . . . I felt as if a great burden had been removed from my mind. It was a beginning, and if not a good one, certainly not a bad one."

Williams also passed and so the two African-American plebes began their first summer at West Point. They soon learned how to march, drill, set up tents, clean equipment, and above all, obey commands instantly during a month-long plebe camp. By the time July 1—the beginning of the academic year—rolled around, they had been transformed from bumbling, inexperienced plebes into what Henry termed, "cadets and gentlemen"; they were now considered fourth classmen.

During the first half of the year, Flipper and Williams studied mathematics, French, artillery and infantry tactics, and fencing, and by January they were ready to be tested. Unfortunately,

Williams failed his examinations and was dismissed, leaving Henry and James Smith as the sole black cadets. Six months later, in June 1874, Smith was also dismissed because of "academic deficiencies." Soon false rumors began to circulate throughout the academy that Henry was also going to leave. In fact, several high-ranking officers approached Henry, urging him to stay and promising him that they would do everything they could to help him graduate. Their gestures reminded Henry that there were some people at the academy who cared about him and wanted to see him succeed.

Having passed his examinations, Henry Flipper was now a third classman, and senior to incoming plebes. Even so, Henry felt extremely alone because the other cadets did not want to associate with the "colored cadet." He recalled, "When I was a plebe those of us who lived on the same floor of barracks visited each other, borrowed books, heard each other recite when preparing for examination, and were really on the most intimate terms. But alas! . . . they learned to call me 'nigger,' and ceased altogether to visit me."

Flipper thought that some of his former plebe friends had been pressured by their relatives or peers to stay away from him. The last thing he wanted to do was to force his friendship on others, so he kept to himself for the next few years.

The worst year for Henry was as a second classman, during his junior year. He remembered the time from October 1875 to May 1876 as "a wretched existence." During that period, he did not speak " . . . to a female of any age." He explained, "There was no society for me to enjoy—no friends, male or female, for me to visit . . . so absolute was my isolation."

Even the holidays weren't happy times for Flipper. "I learned to hate holidays. At those times the other cadets would go off skating, rowing, or visiting. I had nowhere to go except to walk around

The library at West Point

the grounds, which I sometimes did. I more often remained in my quarters. At these times [the] barracks would be deserted and I would get so lonely . . . I wouldn't know what to do," he remarked.

In spite of his loneliness, Henry dug into his studies of philosophy, chemistry, engineering, and military tactics, and continued to improve his horseback riding skills. He reminded himself that "if I cannot endure prejudice and persecutions . . . then I don't deserve the cadetship."

Finally the day Henry had been waiting for arrived: July 1, 1876. On this date, he became a first classman—a senior cadet with privileges. During this time, he also became the focus of several newspaper editorials that tried to predict whether or not he would graduate. Henry paid no attention to the articles and went about enjoying his new status as a senior cadet.

One of the privileges first classmen have is command over other cadets, especially during drills. Orders given by first classmen must be obeyed, otherwise cadets can be reported for insubordination. Even though there were cadets who disliked Henry Flipper, they were forced to do as he said. Many had expected Henry to be tough and unforgiving during drills, considering the type of treatment he had been subjected to as an underclassman. Yet he was surprisingly fair. This earned him a good deal of respect among his peers.

Another thing Flipper enjoyed as a first classman was that he no longer heard himself, either in public or in private, being referred to as "the nigger"; instead, what he heard was "Mr. Flipper."

During his summer as a first classman, Henry was pleased when a plebe came to him openly, seeking advice and friendship. Henry truly thought that his life was taking a new direction and that he might, after all, be accepted among the other cadets.

After several visits, the plebe asked if he could borrow Henry's algebra book to get a head start on his fall studies. Henry obliged, remembering, " . . . I was glad of an opportunity to prove that I was not unkind or ungenerous." Yet, when the plebe returned his book in the fall, Flipper had a far different feeling about this supposed friendship.

The book meant a great deal to Henry; it was one of the ones he had used during his first year at the academy, and he was keeping it as a souvenir. When the book was returned, the leather cover with Henry's name on it had been stripped off, presumably, as Henry remarked, "to conceal

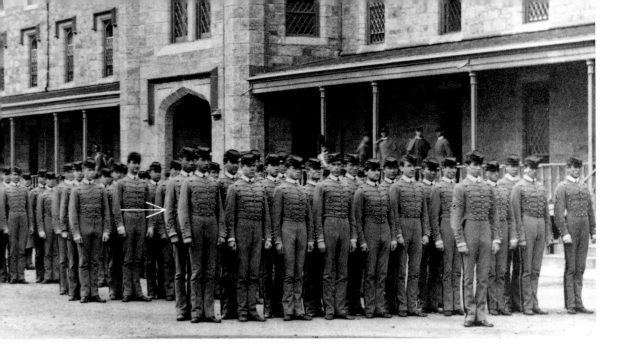

Cadet Flipper
standing in formation
(see arrow)

the fact that [it] was borrowed from me."

By September, Henry's loneliness was eased by the prospect of impending graduation and by the admission of another African American, Johnson Chestnut Whittaker of Camden, South Carolina, who roomed with Henry the remainder of the academic year. (Whittaker never graduated. He was dismissed five years later because of "academic deficiencies.")

As June 1877 approached, Flipper reflected back on his four years at the academy: "They had been years of patient endurance and hard and persistent work . . . with bright oases of happiness . . . as well as weary barren wastes of loneliness [and] isolation." He called his cadet life a "bittersweet experience," saying "I hardly know how I endured it all so long. If I were asked to go over it all again . . . I fear I should fail."

One by one, Henry Ossian Flipper passed his final exams with distinction, showing the rest of the country that an African American was capable of graduating from West Point. His exams in mineralogy and geology, law, civil and military engineering, in ordnance (weaponry), and gunnery received daily attention from the New York newspapers. Oddly, even his fellow cadets congratulated him on the successful completion of his examinations.

"Oh how happy I was!" recalled Flipper. "I prized these good words of the cadets above all others. Several visited my quarters. They did not hesitate to speak to me or shake hands with me before each other . . . . All signs of ostracism were gone."

On June 14, 1877, Cadet Flipper accepted his diploma to a loud round of applause. He was commissioned a second lieutenant in the United States Army and assigned to Troop A of the 10th United States Cavalry. His commission as an officer put him among the army's elite, yet he stood out in a big way. He was the *only* black among the army's 2,100 officers.

Chapter 4

An Important Contribution

After graduation, Lieutenant Flipper went home to Georgia for five months before traveling to his first post, Fort Concho, Texas. His success over prejudice at West Point and the praise he received upon graduation lulled him into believing that his hardest days were over. Henry Flipper had just proven to the country that an African American could overcome racial barriers and become accepted as an officer in the United States Army.

However, upon reaching Atlanta, his home for more than fourteen years, where he "was known by nearly every one in the city," Flipper's reception was lukewarm. "In all the places I visited after graduation," he remarked, "I was treated with the utmost respect and courtesy except in Atlanta. The white people . . . didn't notice me at all. One young man, whom I knew many years . . . hung his head

Lieutenant Flipper's Oath of Office

I, *Henry O Flipper*, having been appointed a *Lieutenant* in the **MILITARY SERVICE** of the **United States**, do solemnly swear that I have never voluntarily **BORNE ARMS** against the United States since I have been a citizen thereof; that I have voluntarily given no **AID, COUNTENANCE, COUNSEL,** or **ENCOURAGEMENT** to persons engaged in **ARMED HOSTILITY** thereto; that I have neither sought, nor accepted, nor attempted to exercise the functions of **ANY OFFICE WHATEVER,** under any authority, or pretended authority, **IN HOSTILITY** to the United States; that I have not yielded a voluntary **SUPPORT** to any **PRETENDED GOVERNMENT, AUTHORITY, POWER,** or **CONSTITUTION WITHIN** the United States, **HOSTILE** or **INIMICAL** thereto. And I do further swear that, to the best of my knowledge and ability, I will **SUPPORT** and **DEFEND** the **CONSTITUTION OF THE UNITED STATES** against all enemies, **FOREIGN** and **DOMESTIC;** that I will bear true **FAITH** and **ALLEGIANCE** to the same; that I take this obligation freely, without any mental reservation or purpose of evasion: and that I will **WELL** and **FAITHFULLY** discharge the **DUTIES** of the **OFFICE** on which I am about to enter: So help me God.

Henry O Flipper
2d Lt 10th Cav'y USA.

Sworn to and subscribed before me, at *Thomasville Ga*
this 21 day of *July* 1877

Jeff Landson JP EC
637 D.G.M.

(A. G. O. No. 55.)

Henry Ware Lawton

and turned away from me, just as I was about to address him on a street in Atlanta."

Henry later commented, "Wherever I have travelled in the South it has been thrown into my face that the Southern people had, would, and did treat me better than the Northern people. This is wholly untrue." He went on to say, " . . . never in a single instance has a Southern man introduced me to his wife or even invited me to his house. It was done North in every place I stopped."

On his way to Fort Concho in December, Henry learned that his troop was now traveling to Fort Sill, Indian Territory, and that he should go there instead. On New Year's Day 1878, Second Lieutenant Henry Flipper proudly arrived at Fort Sill by stagecoach. He was greeted by First Lieutenant Henry Ware Lawton of the 4th Cavalry, who kindly helped him select and furnish his quarters. This warm reception gave Flipper hope that, indeed, he might be treated as an officer and a gentleman.

Since he had arrived a few weeks ahead of his troop, Flipper had a chance to familiarize himself with his new post and to work on his book, *The Colored Cadet at West Point*, that was soon to be published. Flipper was reviewing the previous four years in an autobiographical account based on notes he had taken about his experiences throughout his cadetship. During those early days at Fort Sill, he spent most of his free time writing.

Like most forts of the time, Fort Sill, situated near the eastern end of the Wichita Mountains, was laid out in a large quadrangle with a parade ground in its center. Flanked by several wooded streams, the fort gave the appearance of a neat and orderly post, yet the living conditions were quite primitive. Water for drinking, bathing, and washing had to be obtained from nearby Medicine Bluff Creek. Outhouses were located behind most of the buildings, along with drainage ditches meant to carry away kitchen scraps and refuse. Often these ditches became clogged and smelly and were sources of disease.

Fort Sill had been established ten years earlier to lend support to Indian agents under the government's new Peace Policy, and to keep the nearby Indians from straying from their reservations. In an effort to end fighting among different Indian tribes and between Indians and white settlers, the government set aside millions of acres of land for permanent Indian reservations and promised to provide the Indians with food, clothing, and other supplies. Indian agents were then sent to the reservations to help the Indians adjust to their new lives. In return, the Indians agreed to live peacefully.

One of Henry Flipper's first assignments was to travel to the Wichita Indian Agency, thirty-two miles away, and inspect cattle that were to be given to the Indians. It was humbling experience; Henry ran into testy cowboys who complained of the "nigger officer," and experienced the bitterness of his first midwestern snowstorm. He returned to Fort Sill within twenty-four hours, half frozen in his saddle. He recalled, " . . . my cook, Mrs. Matthews, had to cut my cowhide boots from my feet, how stiff and sore I was . . . "

Soldiers, civilians, and Indians outside the Post Trader's Store at Fort Sill, Indian Territory

From the beginning, Flipper got along extremely well with his troop commander, Captain Nicholas Nolan, an Irishman who seemed to take the young lieutenant under his wing. After arriving at Fort Sill, Nolan traveled to San Antonio, Texas, and got married. He brought his new wife and her sister back to the post with him. "As soon as they were settled," Henry remembered, "Mrs. Nolan insisted that I should board with them. I discharged my cook and did so."

Although the move sparked talk among the soldiers, Henry Flipper was grateful for the friendship and company the Nolans provided. He soon became good friends with the sister, Miss Mollie Dwyer, and the two of them were often seen riding together. "On Sundays," Flipper recalled, "we and other officers and their ladies used to chase coyotes and jackrabbits on the plains. It was great sport, something like fox chasing in England."

Officially, Lieutenant Flipper was the post signal officer, in charge of instructing the troops in military signaling, yet often he performed a number of other duties, including scouting the plains for possible Indian trouble. Flipper's confidence in his work during that first year soared, and he felt comfortable among the other officers stationed at the post. However, the years at West Point had made him independent and somewhat of a loner. Few individuals, if any, knew his deepest thoughts or how he viewed himself as a black officer in a white man's army.

In early 1879, Troop A was ordered to Fort Elliott, Texas; it was a move Henry dreaded, for he had grown so accustomed to Fort Sill. On the day he left the post, he turned around for one last look and wept.

Upon reaching Fort Elliott, Captain Nolan, who was made the commanding officer, appointed Lieutenant Flipper to be his adjutant—a position that Henry described as "the ranking officer on the Commanding Officer's staff . . . . All business is transacted through him," Flipper explained. "If any one wants anything, he must go to the Adjutant." In addition to his adjutant duties, Flipper found time to map and survey the post and to help build a telegraph line from Fort Elliott to Fort Supply in Indian Territory.

Unlike at West Point, Flipper was included in all the social affairs at Fort Elliott. He usually declined invitations to picnics and dances, preferring instead to spend his leisure time riding with Mollie Dwyer.

In November, Flipper's troop returned to Fort Sill. For four months, Henry served as acting captain of Troop G of the 10th Cavalry until the troop's captain, Captain Lee, returned. Lee, a friend of Flipper's, was one of General Robert E. Lee's cousins who had chosen to serve on the Union side during the Civil War.

By March 1880, Henry Flipper's surveying and engineering skills were tested when he was asked to take over the construction of a new road from the post to the railroad station in Gainesville. Flipper did such a terrific job that when the man who had the government freighting contract to haul goods to and from the post rode over the new road, he was so pleased he sent Flipper "a huge barrel filled with all sorts of fine liquors, old whiskeys, brandies, wines and cigars."

A month later, Flipper made his most important contribution to Fort Sill: the construction of a ditch that would drain stagnant pools of water away from the fort. The shallow pools, which extended more than forty miles, were thought to be a source of malaria around the post, causing many soldiers to become sick and die.

Flipper worked for several weeks with the help of a full troop of cavalry regrading the land and

Fort Concho, Texas

digging the ditch. When he had finished, he remembered, " . . . the Commanding Officer and other officers went down to look it over. We got in the ditch and the General told me I had it running up hill and that the grade was wrong. It certainly looked that way, but I knew I was right." The rains proved Henry correct, and water never pooled again. In honor of the African-American lieutenant, the ditch was christened "Flipper's Ditch," and is now a national historic landmark.

By the end of May, Troop A had orders once again to leave Fort Sill; this time their new post was Fort Concho, Texas. Soon after arriving, Troop A joined other troops of the 9th and 10th Cavalries

44

in a military campaign against Indian chief Victorio and his band of Warm Springs Apaches. Victorio and his group were wreaking havoc throughout Texas and New Mexico, stealing and killing wherever they went. They were extremely angry over the government's decision to move them off their New Mexico reservation and place them on a foreign reservation in Arizona. Flipper and his troop went into the field, scouting for signs of Victorio and using old Fort Quitman as their base. When they received word that Victorio's group was in the vicinity, Captain Nolan dispatched Flipper and two other men to travel to Eagle Springs, Texas, to give the news to General Benjamin F. Grierson, the commanding officer of the 10th Cavalry.

Chief Victorio

Henry recalled, "I rode 98 miles in 22 hours mostly at night, through a country the Indians were expected to traverse . . . . I felt no bad effects from the hard ride till I reached the General's tent. Then I attempted to dismount . . . I fell from my horse to the ground, waking the General." After he relayed Nolan's message, Henry fell fast asleep on the ground, using his saddle as a pillow.

Several months later Victorio and his group were cornered by the Mexican cavalry in Mexico. Flipper was sent to a new post—Fort Davis, Texas.

Chapter 5

Clouds on the Horizon

When Lieutenant Flipper reached Fort Davis in the fall of 1880, he became the post quartermaster and the acting "commissary of subsistence," which meant that he was in charge of housing, supplies, and equipment for the entire fort. For example, when an officer needed another wagon or more food for his troops, he contacted Henry Flipper. After each transaction, Flipper detailed how his supplies were used and how much money was spent.

Unlike Fort Sill, which is on the prairie, Fort Davis is situated at the mouth of a rocky, horseshoe-shaped canyon in the eastern end of the Davis Mountains. The post had been established in the mid-1850s to protect settlers, mail carriers, and freighters traveling westward along the road to El Paso. The hilly terrain of the region made traveling difficult, and passing stagecoaches often became targets of raiding Comanches and Apaches. For this reason, the soldiers sent to Fort Davis spent a good deal of time patrolling the San Antonio-El Paso road, scouting for possible trouble with the Indians.

Flipper adapted quickly to life at the remote fort and to his new responsibilites. Within months, he was receiving praise from his fellow officers for his handling of his commissary duties. Even the local merchants liked the way the young, black lieutenant did business; he was honest and trust-worthy.

Yet clouds began to appear on the horizon as early as January 1881. Although he was able to continue riding with his dear friend Mollie Dwyer, Flipper soon became aware of a growing jealousy among several officers over their unique relation-ship. His neighbor, First Lieutenant Charles Nordstrom, seemed particularly jealous and even-tually wooed Miss Dwyer away from Flipper.

The next blow came in March when Colonel Shafter took over command of the fort. Shafter had a reputation for harassing any officers he dis-liked. Almost immediately, Shafter stripped Lieu-tenant Flipper of his quartermaster duties and

"I was afraid to consult the Commanding Officer or any other officer of the post, because of my peculiar situation, because I had heard frequent stories from civilians about the post that the officers there were plotting to get me out of the Army..."

informed him that he would soon be replaced as commissary officer as well.

Shafter then asked Flipper to move the commissary funds from the quartermaster's safe to Flipper's quarters. It was an unusual request, but the lieutenant complied with the colonel's wishes. Four months later, in July, as Henry was going over his commissary statements, he discovered a shortage of $2047.26. Although he knew that two to three hundred dollars were owed by various soldiers, he had no idea where the rest of the money had gone.

He later explained, "I was afraid to consult the Commanding Officer or any other officer of the post, because of my peculiar situation, because I had heard frequent stories from civilians about the post that the officers there were plotting to get me out of the Army, and because I had seen . . . other officers prowling around my quarters at unseemly hours of the night. I so conducted myself as to be perfectly secure against any of their attacks. Up to that moment I never dreamed that anything was wrong with my commissary funds beyond the discrepancy of $200 or $300."

Henry Flipper suspected foul play, but decided to keep the matter to himself, resolving to make up the difference with his own money. His plan almost succeeded. However, while Flipper was waiting for a check from his book publisher to cover the missing funds, the chief commissary of the Department of Texas contacted Shafter, asking why July's money had not been deposited as usual in the bank in San Antonio. Colonel Shafter decided to investigate.

On August 13, 1881, Shafter sent two officers to Henry Flipper's quarters to search for the missing commissary funds. As the officers rifled through his personal belongings, Flipper stood by helplessly. When the officers were done, they seized commissary statements and checks, along with Flipper's West Point class ring.

Later that evening, Shafter accused the army's only black officer of embezzling government funds and arrested him, confining Flipper to the felons' cell in the guardhouse. The cell was so tiny that the "slats of the bunk had to be cut off to permit it to go in." Colonel Shafter prohibited anyone from visiting the cell without his approval, and at first he denied Lieutenant Flipper bedding, books, and writing materials.

Word soon spread throughout the settlement about Henry Flipper's incarceration, and the residents quickly began collecting money to cover the missing funds. By the morning of August 15, almost $1,700 had been collected. When three friends were allowed to visit Fliper later that day, he learned of the townspeoples' generosity and their belief that he was innocent of any wrongdoing.

Colonel Shafter hinted that if Flipper's friends were able to collect enough money, he might drop all charges. Full restitution of the $2,047.26 was quickly made, and Henry Flipper was released to his quarters on August 17, four days after his arrest.

The guardhouse (foreground) and barracks (background) at Fort Davis

Yet Henry's troubles were far from over.

Henry recalled, "After being released from the guardhouse, I was contained in my quarters, which were barricaded, nailed up, and made as secure as the guardhouse was, and was guarded day and night by an armed sentinel." Flipper also discovered that while he had been locked in the guardhouse, his quarters had been further searched, and several personal items had been taken. Shortly afterward, even though all the missing money had been repaid, Shafter brought court-martial charges against the second lieutenant.

When the court-martial convened on September 17, 1881, in the Fort Davis chapel, Henry Flipper found himself with no representation and facing a ten-member court-martial board, three of whom worked directly under Shafter. Lieutenant Flipper quickly asked for a temporary postponement so that he could raise money to hire a lawyer for his defense. A delay was granted.

Henry soon discovered that no lawyer would take his case for less than one thousand dollars, so he sent a white friend east to try to raise money for his defense. In Washington, Boston, New York, and Philadelphia, his friend met with the leading African Americans of the day and explained all the details of Henry's case. However, no one offered to help.

Time was running out, when, as Flipper later wrote, "like a bolt out of a clear sky, I received a letter from Captain Merritt Barber of the 16th U.S. Infantry, white, offering to come and defend me. I had never seen or heard of him before, but . . . I accepted his offer at once, especially as I knew it would cost me nothing, officers not being allowed to charge anything for defending another."

"He came," Flipper continued, "lived in my

Captain Merritt Barber

quarters with me and made a brilliant defense, better than any civilian lawyer could have done. But I was doomed beforehand." As it turned out, the prosecuting attorney also happened to be the Judge Advocate General in Texas, whose role it was to select the officers of the court and review all court proceedings after trials. He would then approve or disapprove of the court's findings. He also happened to be a white captain with the black 24th Infantry, which Flipper thought was a terrible "irony of fate."

The chapel at Fort Davis

The court-martial lasted until December 8, with Barber successfully bringing forth a string of witnesses testifying to Lieutenant Flipper's integrity, while also exposing inconsistencies in the prosecution's case. The lack of physical evidence proving embezzlement and Colonel Shafter's continued contradictions of his own testimony aided Flipper's case. Barber attributed the disappearance of the funds to Flipper's inexperience in financial matters, stating that "under Shafter's lax command," his responsibilities were too much for Flipper to assume alone.

Nevertheless, the court found Lieutenant Henry Ossian Flipper *not guilty* of embezzlement but *guilty* "of conduct unbecoming an officer and gentleman," and sentenced him to be "dismissed from the service of the United States." It was a harsh sentence. In two prior cases involving white officers who were found guilty of embezzlement, neither officer was dismissed nor dishonored.

Henry Flipper's case was reviewed by several high-ranking officials, one of whom recommended to the Secretary of War that Flipper's sentence be reduced to a lesser punishment. The Secretary of War agreed and sent word to President Chester A. Arthur recommending a lighter sentence.

However, for some unknown reason, the president ignored the plea for leniency, and on June 24, 1882, he confirmed the court's original decision to dismiss Lieutenant Flipper from the army. Six days later, Second Lieutenant Henry Flipper was dishonorably discharged.

Chapter 6

A New World

Disgraced, Flipper sold his horses and army equipment and went to El Paso. He soon found temporary work in a steam laundry, while he attempted to adjust to his new life. "I was thoroughly humiliated, discouraged, and heart-broken at the time," he recalled. Yet, "I preferred to go forth into the world and by my subsequent conduct as an honorable man and by my character disprove the charges."

In the fall of 1883, a former Confederate soldier named A. Q. Wingo, whom Henry had met a few years earlier while surveying in Texas, had just been hired by an American company to survey large tracts of public lands in Mexico. Wingo asked that the company hire Flipper to be his assistant. It was the break Henry needed. "I was employed," Flipper wrote, "but before I could go, I was notified

Henry Flipper, shortly after his discharge from the Army

there was some objection because of my race. They wrote their objections to Wingo and proposed another man, a white man. Wingo told them to send me or send a man to take his place. I was hurried down to him without any more ado."

"I was in a new world," Flipper said, when he arrived in Chihuahua, Mexico, to meet up with Wingo. Although he spoke Spanish fairly well, Flipper was not prepared for the poverty he found in Chihuahua. There were no hotels or restaurants in the town of 22,000 people, and there was only one school and that was for boys. Girls were not permitted to go to school.

After being officially appointed surveyors, Flipper and Wingo traveled forty miles south to the small town of Santa Rosalia, where they bought supplies and mules for their journey into the desert. They also hired some Mexican workers, as well as a cook. In November they set off across the hot, flat country, working for the next several years mapping various sections of Mexico.

Once, while Flipper was working by himself near Yuma, Arizona, he arranged to board with an American couple who were farming near the border. "One day," Flipper recalled, "when [the wife] and I were alone at the table, she asked me if I knew who she was. Of course, I had to say I did not. Then she startled me by saying: 'I am a niece of Jefferson Davis . . . . ' Think of that! A niece of Jefferson Davis cooking and washing for a Negro and eating at the same table with him, working for him for wages!" Jefferson Davis was the President of the Confederate States during the Civil War.

It wasn't until 1887 that Flipper decided to settle down near the town of Nogales, Arizona, close to the Mexican border. He had recently been hired by the Sonora Land Company of Chicago to be their chief engineer, and he opened an office for the company in the town. During this period, he also found time to fill in for the publisher of the *Nogales Sunday Herald* for four months in his absence.

Flipper was very familiar with Mexican and Spanish laws regarding land ownership because of his engineering work, so when the townspeople of Nogales needed someone to represent them in a land-grant case before the Court of Private Land Claims, they hired Flipper. Flipper's expert testimony helped to save the property of hundreds of Nogales' landowners and eventually won him an appointment as a special agent for the Department of Justice in 1893.

While working as a special agent, Henry Flipper spent many hours surveying land claims and translating Mexican and Spanish land laws into English. His skill as a translator was highly praised, and he often traveled to Washington, D.C., to help United States Attorney Matthew Reynolds argue various cases. To Reynolds, Flipper was "efficient, competent, reliable and trustworthy." The Justice Department eventually published Flipper's translations of land laws, which were then used extensively by the United States Supreme Court.

On one of his trips to Washington, Flipper met Barney M. McKay, an ex-sergeant of the 9th Cavalry who had been denied reenlistment into the army after sixteen years of service. McKay was fighting his own battle with the army when he persuaded Flipper to begin an attempt to have his duty and rank in the army restored. Flipper recalled, "I hadn't done anything at that time, although I was preparing to move in the matter."

In 1898, with McKay's help, Henry had a bill introduced to Congress by Congressman Michael Griffin of Wisconsin to clear his army record. This was the way the reinstatement process worked at the time. It was only the first of many bills that went nowhere once they reached the Committee on Military Affairs. When General Joe Wheeler, a congressman from Alabama, heard of Flipper's ordeal, he declared: "That is the damndest outrage I ever heard of and I pledge you my word to make your case a personal case and to push it through the House." Unfortunately, the next day Wheeler was sent to Cuba to fight in the Spanish-American War, and that was the last Flipper ever heard from him. Flipper also offered his services to the United States Army at the start of the war, but recalled, "my telegram was never answered."

Shortly after the turn of the century, Flipper completed his work with the Justice Department and accepted a position as a resident engineer with the Balvanera Mining Company in western Chihuahua, Mexico. When the company was sold, Flipper received a telegram from the new vice president, Albert Fall, asking that he stay on in their legal department, which he did. It was a very wise decision.

Fourteen years later, Albert Fall, by then a United States senator, hired Flipper as a Spanish translator and interpreter for the Senate's Committee on Foreign Relations. When Fall was appointed Secretary of the Interior, he asked Flipper

"I have worked hard at all times to have my Army record cleared but I have never had any illusions and have none now. It is uphill work."

to be his assistant on the International Alaskan Engineer Commission. Flipper accepted the position and used his engineering skills in helping to develop an Alaskan railway system.

While in Washington, Henry Flipper continued working with Barney McKay, attempting to get Flipper's marred military record changed. At the time he wrote, "I have worked hard at all times to have my Army record cleared but I have never had any illusions and have none now. It is uphill work." In 1922, when another bill seemed to die in the Committee on Military Affairs, Flipper finally turned to Fall for help. Fall was good friends with President Warren G. Harding, and Henry appealed to Fall to discuss his case with the president. "My whole soul is in this matter as you know," Henry stated.

Fall wrote a detailed letter to the chairman of the military affairs committee, Senator James W. Wadsworth, extolling Flipper's character and adding that, "Without any hesitancy or qualification whatsoever, I can say to you that he is one of, if not the highest class colored whom I ever met in my life."

After receiving Fall's letter, Wadsworth forwarded it to the Secretary of War, John W. Weeks.

Henry Flipper in 1923

Unfortunately, Weeks knew nothing of Flipper's case and denied Fall's request to reinstate Flipper or to place him on the army's retired list. After learning of Weeks' inaction, Fall vowed that he would make an appeal to the president himself. Before doing so, however, he resigned from his post as Secretary of the Interior in March of 1923.

Flipper also resigned at that time and with Fall's help was hired as chief engineer for the Pantepec Oil Company in Caracas, Venezuela. During the next seven years, Henry Flipper worked as a troubleshooter for the company and translated a Spanish book on combustible minerals for Pantepac.

By 1930, seventy-four-year-old Henry Flipper finally decided it was time to retire and return to the United States. On his way home, Henry stopped in Washington, D.C., to try for the ninth time to change the outcome of that fateful day at Fort Davis forty-eight years earlier. Unsuccessful, Flipper gave up and headed south to Georgia.

Settling with his brother Joseph and his family in their Atlanta home, Flipper continued to keep to a daily routine of rising early and working all day in the study, writing and answering letters. He rarely left the house.

On the morning of April 26, 1940, when the family cook arrived to start breakfast, she had to ring the doorbell twice—something she had never had to do before. Flipper always greeted her on the first ring. When Joseph Flipper's stepson, Charles Rembert, finally opened the door, the two realized that something must be wrong. A few minutes later, they found Flipper almost dressed for the day—with the exception of one shoe—lying across his bed, dead of a heart attack. Henry Ossian Flipper was eighty-four years old.

Flipper's passing went unnoticed by most of the major newspapers that had so loudly trumpeted his success at West Point in 1877. The three exceptions were the *New York Herald* and two Atlanta daily newspapers. His burial in an unmarked grave in Atlanta's Southview Cemetery caused one friend from the *Atlanta Daily World* to remark, "He died unwept, unhonored, unsung." Yet, in filling out his death certificate, his brother Joseph gave "him in death what had been taken from him in life," one historian wrote. In the spaces for name and occupation, Joseph wrote, "Lieutenant Henry O. Flipper," and "Retired Army Officer."

"He died unwept, unhonored, unsung."

Chapter 7

Righting a Terrible Wrong

In Valdosta, Georgia, thirty years after Henry Flipper's death, a white student at Valdosta State College named Ray MacColl came across accounts of Flipper's case while working on a term paper about African Americans in the Old West. Although he only mentioned Flipper briefly in his paper, MacColl was intrigued and wanted to find out more about this unusual man. "Flipper's story kept coming to me," MacColl said. "I had no particular purpose in the beginning. I just started reading more and more about him." After graduating from college and starting a career as a teacher, MacColl continued to collect information about West Point's first black graduate and soon became convinced that Flipper's court-martial had been mishandled and that his punishment had been too severe.

MacColl was put in touch with Irsle King, Flipper's niece, who also lived in Valdosta. "I met Mrs. King in October 1974," said MacColl. "We had talked over the phone beforehand, and she seemed very friendly." "When I opened the door," Irsle King recalled of their first meeting, "he actually felt like kin to me. Our spirits agreed as one, as old folks say." With the help of King and other Flipper relatives, MacColl pieced together portions of the forgotten history of Second Lieutenant Henry Ossian Flipper.

Irsle King remembered visiting her uncle during his final years: "To me, he was a military man to the very end. He was quite erect for his age; he never slumped, and he didn't shuffle about. And he was so punctual about everything. The Lieutenant would talk about the court-martial, but get off the subject quickly. He didn't have any hatred, but he had so much regret because he felt mistreated."

MacColl, together with King, decided that they would make a final attempt to restore Flipper's good name. It was something Irsle King had always wanted to do, and she sensed that Ray MacColl was the one to do it. "Mrs. King gave me the inspiration, the desire, to clear his name," MacColl

explained. "The mistake had to be corrected, and I had the commitment to see it through."

In addition to the Flipper relatives, MacColl discovered other individuals throughout the country who were as interested in Flipper's case as he was and who were also anxious to see Flipper's records changed. In Thomasville, Georgia, where Henry Flipper was born, historian Tom Hill was the first individual to get MacColl actively involved, telling him where to look for information and what steps to take if he was truly serious about changing history. Hill, in turn, introduced MacColl to Thomasville lawyer Roy Lilly, Jr., who would later help MacColl shape his findings into a persuasive legal argument. During this time, MacColl wrote to his congressman, Dawson Mathis, who gave MacColl advice on who he should contact in the government and the procedures he should follow in dealing with the army. And in Washington, D.C., the late Sarah Dunlap Jackson, a historian at the National Archives, offered more advice and information.

"It was like a jigsaw puzzle," MacColl said, "trying to connect all these people and their thoughts." Historians Steve Wilson and Bruce Dinges in Oklahoma and Arizona added various

Irsle King and Ray MacColl

pieces to MacColl's puzzle. When Commander Wesley A. Brown, the first black graduate of the U.S. Naval Academy who had once written a paper on Flipper, found out about MacColl's crusade, he introduced him to H. Minton Francis, the eighth black graduate of West Point and the man MacColl credits as playing the most important role in the effort to clear Henry Flipper's name.

Using Flipper's own arguments, MacColl prepared his appeal to the Army Board for Correction of Military Records. His main argument was that if Henry Flipper had been found innocent of embezzling government funds, then he should not have been found guilty of improper conduct. He contended that the second charge was dependent upon the first—the embezzlement charge.

After six months of reviewing MacColl's argument and the Army's own official records, the board decided that Flipper never intended to defraud the government. Since he did replace the missing funds, the board agreed that his sentence should have been less severe. On December 13, 1976, the board reversed the ninety-four-year-old decision and recommended that the army grant Second Lieutenant Henry Ossian Flipper an honorable discharge, dated June 30, 1882, which it did.

Upon hearing the good news, Irsle King commented: "My only regret is that my uncle wasn't around to know that he was cleared. But sometimes we can have the strangest feelings about things. I have always felt like somehow he knew. Maybe it was the satisfaction in my heart that caused me to feel that way." When she finally received the honorable discharge papers in the mail, she recalled, " . . . it felt very, very good . . . it seemed that a burden was lifted from my very soul."

Ray MacColl was also relieved. His hard work had paid off, and the terrible wrong that he had come across seven years earlier had now been righted. The army's reversal did not go unnoticed by the military academy at West Point. The following year the academy celebrated the one hundredth anniversary of Flipper's graduation. The superintendent of the academy designated February 10 "Henry O. Flipper Day."

On that day, a permanent display to honor the academy's first black graduate was established in the West Point library. Included in the memorial is a bust of Lieutenant Flipper, created by a noted African-American sculptress, Helene M. Hemmans. When the display was dedicated, the superintendent of the academy commented that

The bust of Henry Flipper in the West Point library

"there was a strength and gentleness [in Flipper] that transcended any bad treatment [he] received." After the dedication, a parade was held in Flipper's honor. And every year in February, West Point hosts the Henry Flipper Memorial Dinner in recognition of its first black graduate.

On June 7, 1977, the first annual Henry O. Flipper award was presented to a graduating cadet "who best [typified] the attributes of Flipper . . . leadership, self-discipline, and perseverance displayed in the face of unusual difficulties while a cadet." The award was presented by Irsle King's grandson, Lieutenant William R. Davis, a 1976 graduate of the United States Air Force Academy.

In 1978, Ray MacColl and Irsle King joined forces again and had Henry Flipper's remains exhumed from his unmarked grave in Atlanta and moved to Thomasville. On February 11, five hundred friends, relatives, and government officials gathered at the First Missionary Baptist Church to pay their respects and listen to H. Minton Francis eulogize an extraordinary African-American soldier. Francis said that Henry Flipper "epitomized every black man of courage."

Afterward, a military honor guard from Fort Benning, Georgia, led the procession from the church to the Old Magnolia Cemetery. Flipper's casket, draped with an American flag, was carried in a mule-drawn wagon that was followed by a riderless horse, as is customary in certain military funerals. The horse signifies that a cavalry officer has fallen. At the cemetery, three shots from seven guns were fired simultaneously, honoring Lieutenant Flipper. He was then laid to rest next to his parents.

Henry Flipper's casket is escorted to the Old Magnolia Cemetery

"I'm sure there are dozens of other incredible people out there who have been overlooked. And folks like me searching for them. That's the only way people who are lost in the pages of history are going to have their stories told."

Another ceremony was held at Flipper's gravesite in 1987. This time, a state historical marker was unveiled, noting Henry Flipper's place in America's military history. And since 1985, MacColl and King have been trying to get the United States Postal Service to issue a Henry Flipper stamp. So far, no postage stamp has been issued recognizing any African-American soldier. MacColl is confident that such a stamp will soon be commissioned, and he feels the honor should go to Flipper, as the first African-American graduate of the country's oldest and most prestigious service academy.

Looking back on his efforts to clear Flipper's name and bring his past accomplishments to light, Ray MacColl explained, "I never thought my interest would lead to something like this . . . because I was totally unprepared by background. Henry Flipper had been overlooked all those years. History is such a big, big thing, full of holes and footnotes. I'm sure there are dozens of other incredible people out there who have been overlooked. And folks like me searching for them. That's the only way people who are lost in the pages of history are going to have their stories told."

During his 1977 speech at the dedication of West Point's permanent memorial to Flipper, the superintendent of the academy called Henry Ossian Flipper "a trailblazer in the Army's equal rights struggle for blacks." And, indeed, Flipper helped pave the way for African Americans in all branches of the military. By enduring ostracism and racism, Flipper showed the nation that blacks could overcome any obstacles set before them. His courage is an example for all African Americans.

Chronology:

African Americans in the U.S. Armed Forces

1770	On March 5, Crispus Attucks, a former slave, is among the first to die in the "Boston Massacre."
1776-1781	7,000 African-American soldiers and sailors take part in the Revolutionary War.
1776	On January 16, the Continental Congress agrees to enlist free blacks.
1812-1815	Black soldiers and sailors fight against the British troops at such critical battles as Lake Erie and New Orleans.
1862-1865	186,000 African-American soldiers serve in black regiments during the Civil War; 38,000 black soldiers lose their lives in more than 400 battles.
1862	On July 17, the U.S. Congress approves the enlistment of black soldiers.
1865	On March 13, the Confederate States of America begins to accept black recruits.
1866-1890	Units of black soldiers, referred to as Buffalo Soldiers, are formed as part of the U.S. Army.
1872	On September 21, John H. Conyers becomes the first African American admitted to the U.S. Naval Academy.
1877	On June 15, Henry O. Flipper becomes the first African American to graduate from West Point.
1914-1918	More than 400,000 African Americans serve in the U.S. armed forces during the First World War.

On May 15, two black soldiers, Henry Johnson and Needham Roberts become the first Americans to receive the French Medal of Honor (*croix de guerre*).	1918
In June, Benjamin O. Davis, Jr., graduates from West Point, the first black American to do so in the twentieth century.	1936
Benjamin O. Davis, Sr., becomes the first African-American general in the active Regular Army.	1940
American forces in World War II include more than a million African-American men and women.	1941-1945
On March 25, the Army Air Corps forms its first black unit, the 99th Pursuit Squadron.	1941
On August 24, Colonel Benjamin O. Davis, Jr., is made commander of the 99th Pursuit Squadron.	1942
On January 27 and 28, the airmen of the 99th Pursuit Squadron score a major victory against enemy fighters at the Italian seaside town of Anzio.	1944
On February 2, President Harry S Truman signs Executive Order 9981, ordering an end to segregation in the U.S. armed forces.	1948
Black and white forces fight side by side in Korea as separate black fighting units are disbanded.	1950-1953
Twenty African-American soldiers are awarded the Congressional Medal of Honor during the Vietnam War.	1965-1973
On April 28, Samuel L. Gravely becomes the first black admiral in the history of the U.S. Navy.	1971
In August, Daniel "Chappie" James becomes the first African American to achieve the rank of four-star general.	1975
On October 3, Colin Powell becomes the first African-American chairman of the Joint Chiefs of Staff.	1989
100,000 African-American men and women are sent to the Middle East during the Persian Gulf conflict.	1990-1991
On July 25, the Buffalo Soldier Monument is dedicated at Fort Leavenworth, Kansas.	1992

Index

References to photographs are listed in ***italic, boldface*** type.

Bibliography

Black, Lowell D., and Sara H. Black. *An Officer and a Gentleman: The Military Career of Henry O. Flipper*. Dayton, Ohio: The Lora Company, Ltd., 1985.

Dinges, Bruce. "Court-Martial of Lieutenant Henry O. Flipper: An Example of Black-White Relationships in the Army, 1881." *The American West*, January 1972.

Flipper, Henry Ossian. *The Colored Cadet at West Point*. New York: Homer Lee & Co., 1878.

Harris, Theodore, ed. *Negro Frontiersman: The Western Memoirs of Henry O. Flipper*. El Paso: Texas Western College Press, 1963.

Maraniss, David. "Due Recognition and Reward." *The Washington Post Magazine*, January 20, 1991.

McPherson, James M. *Battle Cry of Freedom*. New York: Ballantine Books, 1988.

Nye, Colonel W. S. *Carbine & Lance: The Story of Old Fort Sill*. Norman, Oklahoma: University of Oklahoma Press, 1969.

Utley, Robert M. *Fort Davis National Historic Site, Texas*. Washington, D.C.: National Park Service Historical Handbook Series No. 38, 1965.

—. *Frontier Regulars: The United States Army and the Indian, 1866–1891*. Lincoln: University of Nebraska Press, 1973.

Wakin, Edward. *Black Fighting Men in U.S. History*. New York: Lothrop, Lee & Shepard Co., 1971.

Ward, Geoffrey C. *The Civil War: An Illustrated History*. New York: Alfred A. Knopf, 1990.

Wilson, Steve. "A Black Lieutenant in the Ranks." *American History*, December 1983.